A LITTLE HOPE

BY MARY FLEESON

Hope gives us a reason to live,
a purpose beyond the ordinary
day-to-day existence.
Let us explore together what a
difference hope makes...

In you, Lord my God, I put my trust.

The Psalms are a great reminder that humans throughout time have striven to understand their place in the universe and their relationship with God.

Even Kings, prophets and leaders of nations have despaired and lost hope but the more they have railed at God, shouted and cried, the more they have confirmed their belief in their Creator and the more they accept their belief, the more hope has become a viable option!

When we moved to the Island we found ourselves without an income, with a doubled mortgage and up to our eyes in debt. We brought forward plans to open a Christian Bookshop and muddled along, often we would have just exactly the right amount of money scraped together for a food shop - down to the last penny. Our struggle will be familiar to many and we, like the Psalmists of old cried and shouted to God, "Why? We are doing what You called us to do!" We even questioned if God actually existed!

Eventually we realised that despite it all we were still communicating with God, we were praying, not in the most calm and measured way but it was still prayer. And if we believed in God enough to yell then we were hoping that the same God was listening. Hope conquered despair.

HOPE

Now, at this moment, I put my trust in You.
Today, and all my days, I will put my hope in You.

In my dark times I will seek Your face.
In my settled times I will not forget to pray.

PRAY

My hope, Lord, is in you

Psalm 25 v1

LOVE GOD WITH ALL YOUR HEART
AND WITH ALL YOUR SOUL
AND WITH ALL YOUR MIND
AND WITH ALL YOUR STRENGTH.

A NEW COMMAND I GIVE YOU:
LOVE ONE ANOTHER.
AS I HAVE LOVED YOU,
SO YOU MUST LOVE
ONE ANOTHER.

JESUS SAID,
"FOLLOW ME"

I wait for the Lord,
my whole being waits,
and in His word
I put my hope.

Psalm 130:5

After the shouting and crying came a sense of expectation, the 'word' that we took hope in was the calling we had to be on the Island.

There are some things we are all called to do, each day we can ask ourselves:

HOW DO I... love God

_____
_____
_____

HOW DO I... love others

_____
_____
_____

HOW DO I... follow Jesus

_____
_____
_____

Some days you will find you can answer clearly, some days the question will hang there waiting to be answered. Rest in either response and wait for an answer or for the next step to be revealed.

P Help me to love You more,
even when I cannot sense Your presence.
R Help me to love others unconditionally,
especially those I don't really like.
A Help me to follow the path Jesus trod,
Y even when it takes me to unexpected places.

Show me Your ways...
As we travel further through this journey
called 'Life' we inevitably experience
times when the path is hidden, we have
a decision to make but we're not hearing
what God has to say about it.

This can be extremely distressing,
particularly if, up until that point,
we have been confident that we were
doing exactly what we should be doing
and were in the place we should be,
but, to put it simply, that's life!

There will be ups and downs, twists
and turns, highs and lows...

Show me Your ways, Lord, teach me Your paths. Guide me in Your truth and teach me, for you are God my Saviour, and my hope is in you all day long.

Psalm 25:4-5

The ups and downs, twists and turns, highs and lows, can't be avoided, all we can do is learn how to manage them:

with the help of the Spirit,

> the Holy Spirit, whom the Father will send in my name, will teach you all things

> John 14:26

with prayer,

> Father, hallowed be your name,
> your kingdom come.
> Give us each day our daily bread.
> Forgive us our sins, for we also forgive
> everyone who sins against us.
> And lead us not into temptation.

> Luke 11:2-4

with love,

> "As I have loved you,
> so you must love one another."

> John 13:34

and with hope,

> Blessed are those whose help is the God
> of Jacob, whose hope is in the Lord their God.

> Psalm 146:5

Infinite God –
help me to hope fearlessly

"Therefore encourage one another
and build each other up."

1 Thessalonians 5:11

Many moons ago I participated in CMS 'Action Holidays', specifically a two week mission called Wandering Minstrels that used street theatre to evangelise. Over the five Summers that I was involved, one of the most uplifting activities that we used to help the teams bond was to tell each other what we admired about them - at the start it might be 'I like your taste in clothes' or 'I like your smile', towards the end of the mission it could be 'I love how you always make time to listen' or 'I appreciate your humour'.

Sometimes a negative comment can stay with us for years, it can knock our confidence and stunt our hope for the future by making us fear that we are not worthy of a positive/happy/thriving life - an encouraging word however will always have the opposite effect.

I'm not suggesting that we need to be continually feeding our egos by seeking affirmation, more that we should be aware that our looking for the good things in each other is good for us and good for the Kingdom of God, with positive encouragement we are more able to accept the challenge of living fully as Spirit-filled children of God and hoping fearlessly in God's promises - in that place we are equipped to change the world through fearless prayer and action!

Have I not commanded you? Be strong and courageous. Do not be afraid; do not be discouraged, for the Lord your God will be with you wherever you go.
Joshua 1:9

The Lord will watch over your coming and going both now and forevermore.
Psalm 121:8

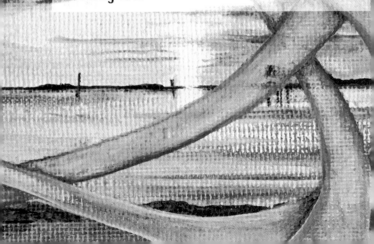

PRAY

To You, my Maker
I offer You the parts of me that I have made...

My fear,
take it, and hone it to be simply wise caution,
rather than a crippling darkness
that overwhelms me.

My limitations,
the ones I put on myself through self doubt,
and the ones I put on You by doubting
Your power.

My walls,
break down the ones that give me a false security,
and the ones that stop me from truly
knowing You.

Be strong and take heart,
all you who hope in the Lord.
Psalm 31:24

God is our refuge and strength, an ever-present help in trouble. Therefore we will not fear, though the earth give way and the mountains fall into the heart of the sea, though its waters roar and foam and the mountains quake with their surging.

'Take heart' - be encouraged! When our hope is firmly placed in the God of creation, in the teaching and sacrifice of Jesus and the guidance of the Spirit, rather than in the transience and whimsy of the world then our hope becomes a bedrock on which we can build our lives.

Psalm 46:1-3

The refuge platforms on the route of the Pilgrim's Way across the sand flats between the mainland and the Island have saved many lives, they offer an immediate help if you find yourself caught by a swiftly rising incoming tide and will save you even if it was your own fault that you got into difficulties - all you have to do is climb a short ladder.

God is the same... our short ladder to salvation is our admission that we need saving.

Consider the times that we have made our relationship with God more difficult than it should be, the times we've made that short ladder into a tall one... with splinters!

Graceful God, help me to pray
when life is chaotic and time seems to vanish.

Loving God, help me to look for hope
in every situation where I am.

Caring God, help me to pray
when all seems hopeless and I have no solutions.

Merciful God, help me to embody Your hope
in every place where I am.

Be joyful

Being joyful isn't about having a permanent grin on your face or always feeling happy... when I first started to look into what it meant to be a Christian, as a teenager with the accompanying hormone roller-coaster, I found it really difficult to understand what 'joy' meant. I was told it was a deep-down assurance, more lasting than 'happy' and something I could only truly experience with God's help. It took me a long time to realise that joy wasn't something that was affected by mood or even circumstance.

I've learnt not to underestimate the power of mind and body on spirit and I still find the balance between them difficult to achieve but joy is sustained by hope and faith and the love beyond measure of our Creator.

Be patient

Patience in affliction is great advice isn't it? There are probably few of us that could say that we're good at being patient even when we know that it will help us to cope, giving ourselves permission to rest and step back from our usual busyness can feel like giving up or giving in but fighting against the needs of your body or mind will only delay their healing.

Be faithful

Faithfulness in prayer is breathing for the soul, it is our constant communication with God. It isn't something we just do on Sundays or at set times but it is in every conversation, every action and every thought. When we pray constantly, we are inviting God to be in our lives, to nurture us and guide us - what could be better?

Be joyful in
hope,
patient in
affliction,
faithful in
prayer.

Romans 12:12

PRAY

Circle me Creator God.
May I hope joyfully,
Keep me from despair.
May I love freely,
Keep me from indifference.
May I believe expectantly,
Keep me from ignorance.